BOOK OF BEASTS

Ticktock

An Hachette UK Company
www.hachette.co.uk

First published in Great Britain in 2013 by Ticktock,
an imprint of Octopus Publishing Group Ltd
Endeavour House
189 Shaftesbury Avenue
London
WC2H 8JY
www.octopusbooks.co.uk
www.ticktockbooks.co.uk

ISBN 978 1 84898 896 5

A CIP record for this book is available from the British Library

Printed and bound in China

1 3 5 7 9 10 8 6 4 2

Project Editor: Simon Breed   Design: Ian Butterworth
Battle art and spot illustrations: Lee Gibbons   Main beast figures: Colin Ashcroft
Publisher: Tim Cook   Managing Editors: Jo Bourne, Karen Rigden
Production: Peter Hunt
Additional text: Simon Breed, Jo Bourne

BOOK OF BEASTS

Illustrations by

Colin Ashcroft & Lee Gibbons

Text by Giles Sparrow

CONTENTS

CHAPTER 1:

6 MONSTERS OF THE GODS

8 Crimes and Misdemeanours
10 Minotaur
12 Gorgon
14 Xolotl
16 Cyclops
18 Surprise Cyclops Attack
20 Naga
22 Centaur

CHAPTER 2:

24 THE UNDEAD

26 Crimes and Misdemeanours
28 Dracula
30 Fight of the Fiends
32 Jiang Shi
34 Golem
36 Zombie
38 Mummy
40 Frankenstein's Monster

CHAPTER 3:

42 DRAGONS
44 Crimes and Misdemeanours
46 Ljubljana Dragon
48 Chinese Dragon
50 DRAGON BATTLE
52 Lambton Worm
54 Jersey Devil
56 Wyvern

CHAPTER 4:

58 SHAPESHIFTERS
60 Crimes and Misdemeanours
62 Werewolf
64 Selkie
66 Kitsune
68 Skinwalker
70 FOREST FIGHT
72 Banshee

CHAPTER 5:

74 TROLLS, GIANTS AND DEMONS
76 Crimes and Misdemeanours
78 Draug
80 Black Shuck
82 Jotun Frost Giant
84 Krampus
86 Elf
88 WAR OF THE ELVES
90 Troll
92 Glossary
94 Index

CHAPTER 1

Monsters OF THE Gods

Ancient beliefs from around the world tell bone-chilling tales of weird and terrifying creatures with supernatural powers, created by the gods for fun, for fear ... or for revenge! In the jungles of South America, the ruined temples of Greece and the swamps of Southeast Asia, they lie in wait, ready to ambush unwary travellers – so beware these demonic deities and unholy horrors!

Crimes and

3.5

3.0

2.5

2

1.5

1.0

0.5

0.0

MINOTAUR

- Smelling terrible
- Using a double-headed axe in a confined space
- Ambushing and slaughtering

GORGON

- Having hissy fits
- Using a killer gaze to turn men into stone
- Having an unmanageably deadly hairstyle

XOLOTL

- Fooling demons for fun
- Discharging lethal lightning without due consideration
- Giving Aztec children nightmares

Misdemeanours

CYCLOPS

- Scoffing scores of stranded sailors
- Tearing up trees with his bare hands
- Possessing a terrible temper - and awful breath

NAGA

- Spitting venom in public
- Vicious swordplay
- Slashing swimmers

CENTAUR

- Unleashing arrows in a rage
- Being drunk in charge of four legs
- Not having a stable background

MINOTAUR

With a tremendous stench and a ferocious bellow, the enormous minotaur emerges from the darkness of his labyrinth. Imprisoned long ago at the heart of this impossible maze, it once fed on human sacrifices, and still waits to ambush any modern-day traveller foolish enough to cross its path.

WEAPON: Doubly deadly axe

The Minotaur lays waste to all who enter his labyrinth, using brute force or his ferocious double-headed axe. Even the most skilled warriors have fallen before his might. Only brains, not brawn, can outwit him.

Monster in the maze

The Queen of Crete gave birth to the monstrous Minotaur after her husband King Minos angered the gods by refusing to sacrifice a sacred white bull. Horrified, the King imprisoned the brute at the centre of an impenetrable maze beneath his palace at Knossos.

TIP: Unwind twine

If you don't want to get lost in the maze, take a ball of twine. The Greek hero Theseus unwound one to trace his path through the labyrinth and rescue a group of Athenians who were about to be sacrificed.

For the Minoan people of ancient Crete, bulls were sacred. The Minoans risked their lives by performing daring leaps in the bullring.

BEAST RATING

- Enemies: Mortals in its maze
- Threat level   7
- Might in battle   7
- Difficulty of slaying   7
- Total   21

GORGON

Something hisses in the darkness, and a glint of torchlight reflects from a baleful eye. Fighting your instincts, you turn away ... just in time! To meet the Gorgon face-to-face means instant stony death - as the ancient Greek heroes found out, you need to reflect carefully on your approach ...

Evil eye of the Gorgon

A Gorgon's gaze is deadly! Make eye contact and you're instantly turned to stone. The last thing you'll see is the Gorgon's evil eyes, as your body seizes up and your bones become brittle and crack like chalk. You are literally petrified to death!

Serpent locks

A Gorgon's hair is a squirming mass of writhing, venomous snakes - any one of which can deliver a killing bite. Some say the Gorgons were once three beautiful sisters called Stheno, Euryale and Medusa, turned into ghastly monsters by the jealous Greek goddess Athena.

SKILLS: Archery

When they were still human, the Gorgon sisters were **ferocious warriors**, famed for their skill with bow and arrow. Today, they still use a **bow to kill**, but they also have other, far deadlier ways of defending themselves.

TIP:
Use a mirror

That's good advice from the Greek hero Perseus. He took a highly polished **shield** with him when he set out to **confront** the Gorgon Medusa. By looking only at her reflection, he avoided being turned to stone - and **lopped off her head.** If you're planning to track down her sisters, remember that everything's the other way around in a **reflection!**

Death's head

Even when Medusa's head was **cut off**, her gaze kept its **awful power.** Perseus used it to turn a giant sea **monster** to stone. Later, Greeks and Romans used **pictures** of the head to **protect** themselves from **evil.**

BEAST RATING

● Enemies: Heroes	
● Threat level	7
● Might in battle	6
● Difficulty of slaying	9
● Total	22

XOLOTL

A rumble of thunder and a **CRASH** of lightning announce that Xolotl's on his way. This Central American god has a **fearsome** reputation - he crosses the boundary between the worlds of the living and the **dead**, protecting the **souls of dead** Aztecs from **demons**, and guiding them to their resting place in the **underworld**.

Xolotl's skeletal body gives away the fact that he spends half the time in Mictlan, the Aztec realm of the dead.

Solar watchdog

While the souls of **dead Aztecs** only have to travel through the **underworld** once, the Sun has to go there every night. It's Xolotl's job to protect it on its journey, and ensure that the Sun rises again the next morning.

WEAPON: Fire and lightning

As if his mastery of the **underworld** wasn't enough, Xolotl is also the god of fire and **lightning**.

TRACKING: Trick prints

Xolotl can reverse his feet when he walks - a handy trick to leave misleading footsteps and shake off Aztec **demons** on his trail.

Xolotl's dog nose gives him a powerful ability to sniff out threats and track down lost Aztec souls when they stray from the path through the underworld. Even today, nearly 500 years after most of the Aztecs were wiped out, the Mexican hairless dog known as the Xoloitzcuintle is named in his honour.

CYCLOPS

Still crunching the bones of his last victim, the evil-tempered Cyclops lumbers from his cave in search of another meal. These one-eyed giants of Greek myth might not be smart, but they're still strong, fast and **brutal hunters** – find yourself stuck on an island with one, and you'll need all your wits to get away in one piece!

HABITAT: Stinky caves

A damp and smelly cave makes an ideal Cyclops home – they often gather their sheep (and any **prisoners** they're saving for later!) inside for the night, before sealing up the entrance with a rock.

LOCATION: Islands

Cyclopes (that's the plural of Cyclops!) live on small, scattered islands in the Mediterranean Sea. **W**reathed in perpetual mist, they're not on any sea chart, because sailors who find them rarely make it back alive!

TACTIC: Aim for the eye

A Cyclops's single eye is its one weak spot – although these monsters have very sharp vision, they can't judge distance very well. If you can, steel your nerves, flatten yourself against the rock face, and try to keep still – moving will just make you easier to spot. But...

...If a Cyclops does spot you, try to **poke** it in the **eye!** The Greek hero Odysseus used a sharpened stake to blind a Cyclops called Polyphemus, so that he and his stranded crew could **escape** from the island.

Most Cyclops are shepherds and raise large flocks of sheep to eat. But raw mutton every day gets boring after a while, which may be why the tasty human flesh of a shipwrecked sailor is a Cyclop's favourite treat.

WEAPONS:
Basic but big

Despite being pretty dumb, the average Cyclops is very **strong** – they often **rip trees** from the ground, stripping their branches to make a **crude** but effective **club.**

BEAST RATING

- **Enemies: Mortals, Heroes**
- **Threat level** 6
- **Might in battle** 8
- **Difficulty of slaying** 8
- **Total** 24

Surprise Cyclops Attack

Two centaurs are cantering through a treacherous valley when suddenly a massive Cyclops attacks – stabbing at their flanks with a tree trunk! Quick as a flash, the Centaurs let loose their lethal arrows ...

NAGA

Rising from muddy waters comes the terrifying Naga, her **serpent** crests rearing to spit their venom at you before her entire snakelike body **writhes** and **twists** its way onto land! Each member of this race of Asian river **monsters** is **dangerous**, unpredictable and driven by their **voracious** appetites.

Airborne enemy

The sight of an **eagle** soaring overhead will send Naga **slithering** towards the nearest river. These birds of prey are the natural predators of all **snakes**, and even Naga have an instinctive **fear** of them.

WEAPON: Venom

Nagas' human-like heads are crowned with up to seven **serpent** crests that **spit fatal poison**. They are related to the deadly King **Cobras** of India and southeast Asia. In some cases, the crests even have the heads of cobras themselves.

TRACKING: Telltale lights

Along stretches of Thailand's great Mekong River, shoreline villagers and fishermen keep a **wary eye** out for hungry Naga. Glowing **fireballs** that rise from the river reveal the Naga's presence!

BEAST RATING

- Enemies: Those who harm waters
- Threat level   8
- Might in battle   6
- Difficulty of slaying 6
- Total   20

WEAPON: Deadly blades

You might think each Naga was **dangerous** enough without a **weapon**, but Hindu myths tell of their involvement as armed warriors in many **battles**.

Rear propulsion

The Naga's **twisting** tail makes it a powerful **swimmer** – they spend most of their time in water, only emerging onto land to feed. In India they're seen as protectors of wells, springs and rivers – but think twice before going for a swim in **their territory!**

Centaur

All thundering hooves and rattling armour, the Centaur pauses to sniff the air and stamp his foot, before rearing to his full impressive height. This noble but fearsome creature of Greek myth marries the body and legs of a horse, to the torso, head and arms of a man, making him a deadly opponent in battle.

WEAKNESS: Wine

One thing that all Centaurs have in common is their love of wine - they like nothing better than getting drunk and partying. So if you come across a raging Centaur, your best bet may be to keep him drinking until he forgets what made him angry - or just falls asleep!

SKILL: Archery

The Centaurs are famed for their archery skills - sharp eyesight and powerful arms allow them to hit their targets over huge distances. That's why the constellation of Sagittarius, the Archer, is usually shown as a centaur with a bow and arrow.

Wise heads

Some centaurs have risen above their beastly nature. The most famous of all was Chiron, a wise teacher and physician, who taught many Greek heroes, including Perseus and the great warrior Achilles.

Horse-backed warriors

The ancient Greeks knew the Centaurs as **vicious fighters** who descended from the steppe region between Asia and Europe to do **battle** - they were all the more **fearsome** because the Greeks hadn't mastered the art of horse riding.

TACTIC: Trust - just!

Centaurs are smart and think with their human brains, but they sometimes let their **animal side** get the better of them - they can be rude, **untrustworthy**, skittish and quick to **anger** - so even if you come across one that seems friendly, stay on **your guard!**

BEAST RATING

- Enemies: Mortals, other beasts
- Threat level — 7
- Might in battle — 7
- Difficulty of slaying — 6
- Total — 20

23

CHAPTER 2

The Undead

Every country has tales of **horrific** monsters that won't lie down and **die** – ageless, **deathless** and **deadly,** they exist in the **borderland** between the living and the dead. Some are just as **cunning** as when they were **alive,** while others are mindless servants to the creators that **summoned** them back from the **grave.** Either way, it takes a lot of courage to confront these crimes **against nature!**

Crimes and

DRACULA

- Being a pain in the neck
- Stealing blood ... from the living
- Possessing lethal teeth

JIANG SHI

- High hopping without a licence
- Being in dire need of a manicure
- Scaring people witless

GOLEM

- Being a muddy nuisance
- Going on the rampage
- Mindless behaviour

Misdemeanours

ZOMBIE

- Generally being rotten
- Devouring the flesh of the living
- Shedding maggoty flesh in public spaces

MUMMY

- Using curse words
- Making tombs terrifying
- Staying in bed for thousands of years

FRANKENSTEIN'S MONSTER

- Murder
- Being angry with his 'dad'
- Stomping after dark

27

Dracula

At first glance he might seem **handsome** and charming, but you'll need to stay on your guard while **Dracula's** on the loose! Despite appearances, this **undead** nobleman is a savage monster with supernatural powers - and a **thirst for human blood.**

LOCATION: Transylvania

Count Dracula began his life as a Hungarian **warrior** prince, Vlad Tepes of the House of Dracul, famed for his cruel treatment of prisoners, who he **impaled** on **spikes**. No one knows how he won his immortality, but he haunts his Romanian castle to this day, lying in wait for unwary travellers.

Bloodsucker

Vampires like nothing better than **biting** into your neck and **drinking** your blood. They usually prefer to keep you alive, so they'll just take a little at a time. Watch out if you wake up with a pair of strange marks on your throat!

TIPS: Repellents

There are various ways of making a vampire keep its distance. Two traditional ones are: a crucifix (if you don't have one around, making a **cross** from a pair of candlesticks might work), and **garlic** - though eat too much and it might not just be vampires you're **scaring** off!

TACTIC: Check reflections

One sure way of spotting if you're sleeping over at Hotel Dracula is to check on your host's **reflection** - vampires don't show up in **mirrors**.

TO VANQUISH:
Strike in the day!

Vampires might be immortal, but they're not invulnerable; you can kill them by driving a wooden stake through their heart. Ambush them during the day while they're asleep in a coffin.

- Enemies: Mortals
- Threat level — 7
- Might in battle — 7
- Difficulty of slaying — 2
- Total — 16

FIGHT OF THE FIENDS

Deep in the **secret** vaults of an undiscovered Egyptian **tomb**, Vlad Dracula soars in rage past his bloodless foe, only to be ensnared in the **Mummy's bandages!**

JIANG SHI

Hopping along on one foot with its arms outstretched, this Chinese **zombie** might look weird, and even funny – but stand there chuckling and you'll soon see who has the last laugh! These surprisingly fast-moving **living corpses** will **kill** anything that crosses their path in order to absorb their **life force.**

Unfinished business

Unlike the zombies of Haiti, Jiang Shi seem to come back to life on their own – often when a **coffin** is left unburied after the funeral or struck by lightning, or when a **black cat** leaps across the corpse. Their **restless spirits** are often driven by the need to settle unfinished business.

Telltale style and skin

Jiang Shi wear old-fashioned Chinese clothing – they originated in the Qing Dynasty more than 100 years ago, and don't seem to have changed their fashions with the times. Apart from their traditional outfits, the other big clue to a Jiang Shi's spooky nature is the ghastly greenish colour of its decaying skin.

TO VANQUISH: Use seeds!

There are lots of ways to scare off Jiang Shi – apart from roosters, they're scared of their own reflections, items made of peach wood, sticky rice and bells. If you need to finish one off, however, the recommended way is to hammer seven seeds from the Jujube fruit into the acupuncture points on its back – ouch!

A Jiang Shi's body is still as stiff as a board - which is why they hop on one foot with their arms sticking out to keep them balanced.

Night owls

Jiang Shi roam the land **at night,** but fear sunlight and flee to **dark caves** and other hiding places at dawn. If you're venturing into Jiang Shi country, take a rooster with you - Jiang Shi aren't that bright, and they'll often hop off when they hear a cockerel crow, even if it's the middle of the **night!**

BEAST RATING

- **Enemies: Mortals**
- **Threat level**   7
- **Might in battle**   7
- **Difficulty of slaying**   2
- **Total**   16

GOLEM

A roughly finished mass of **crumbling** clay, the Golem is a shambling, foot-dragging **giant** straight out of your worst **nightmares.** Created to protect, its **violent** nature soon got out of control, before it **disappeared** into the **mists** of **history.**

TO DESTROY:
Go for the head

A glowing jewel in the Golem's forehead acts as its **soul** - tug it out and you'll **destroy** the monster for good.

Out of the earth

There have been many **Golems.** The last and most famous was supposed to have been created out of earth and mud by Rabbi Loew in Prague. Like all Golem, this one was a **mindless** servant, **brought to life** to protect the Jews of the city from being **attacked.**

TO VANQUISH:
Pull the paper

Rabbi Loew brought the Golem to life by **stuffing** a piece of paper inscribed with **magic words** into its mouth. Pull the paper out and it turns back to a lump of **clay** - but you'll have to get very close to **reach** it!

Missing – presumed ...?

The Golem was supposed to be locked away in the **attic** of the Prague Synagogue, but there's noting in there today. Perhaps the monster was brought back to **life** and is still **wandering** the world ... ?

The Golem was meant to protect the Jews of Prague, but it went on the rampage, killing at random until the emperor begged Rabbi Loew to deactivate it.

Zombie

The living dead come in all shapes and sizes, but Zombies come from the Caribbean island of Haiti, where their shambling, decaying corpses are conjured back into action to do the will of Voodoo sorcerers. Tireless and impervious to pain, Zombies might not be fast, but they never give up – so be careful not to get a **Zombie** on your trail!

TIP: Shatter the bottle

Voodoo priests called "bokors" conjure Zombies from death using magic spells to trap part of the soul called the "Zombie astral". Once the bokor has trapped the astral in a bottle, the zombie's body has no will of its own – smash the bottle and the control is broken.

Voodoo dolls

Sorcerors make Zombies out of both living and **dead people** using magic voodoo dolls. When a snip of hair or something else belonging to the victim is attached to one of these crude dolls, they're transformed into a puppet with no choice but to obey the bokor's will.

Use your brains!!!

Everyone loves a Zombie movie, but they've spread a lot of myths over the years, and perhaps the most famous is that they have an insatiable **hunger for brains**. In fact, this idea was made up as recently as the 1980s. It's not as if a hungry Zombie will turn its nose up at **fresh brains**, though – but they're not fussy eaters and will be just as happy chewing on your **arm or leg!**

Living dead

Some bokors can turn living people into **Zombies** with a mix of **drugs and potions**. The victim falls into a **deathlike** sleep before reawakening in a **trance** that leaves them with no option but to do their master's will.

TACTIC: Get salty

Some people say that feeding a Zombie with salt can reverse the bokor's spells and send it back to the grave – but good luck getting close enough to stick a spoon in its mouth!

BEAST RATING

- **Enemies:** They'll eat anyone!
- **Threat level**   5
- **Might in battle**   2
- **Difficulty of slaying**   6
- **Total**   13

MUMMY

Accidentally **reanimated** by curious explorers or greedy treasure hunters, the **Mummy** emerges from its tomb to wreak revenge. Tattered **bandages** hold his parched and **ancient body** together, but despite appearances, he's immensely strong, relentlessly hunting down anyone who dares disturb his **eternal sleep.**

Beware of the Dog

Statues and paintings of the jackal god Anubis, guardian of the Egyptian underworld, guard the mummy's **tomb**, often carrying a curse that threatens **grisly death** to all those who **dare enter** ...

Pyramid scheme

Mummies are the preserved **bodies** of Ancient Egyptian kings called "Pharaohs". Early kings built the famous Pyramids as their last resting places, but later ones hid their **tombs** away in the desert sands.

Mummy bindings

Egyptian priests wrapped the body of a dead **pharaoh** in special bandages to preserve his body on its journey to the underworld – they couldn't have known that the same magic would bring him back to life!

TACTIC: Coffin confrontation

The Mummy rests in a huge box called a sarcophagus (it literally means "flesh eater" – yuck!) covered in magical inscriptions. If you're going to confront him, this is the best place to do it.

38

BEAST RATING

- Enemies: Mortals, Vampires
- Threat level   7
- Might in battle   7
- Difficulty of slaying   7
- Total   21

WEAKNESS: Body parts

The first thing a **resurrected** Mummy will do is to try to pull himself together, tracking down the special "canopic jars" where the priests put his **brain**, heart and other **organs**. He only gains his full strength when he's whole.

THE EGYPTIAN BOOK OF THE DEAD is written on tomb walls and on sarcophagi. If a Mummy's on the rampage, it's got all the spells you need to put him back in his box!

FRANKENSTEIN'S MONSTER

Lurching out of the darkness, **electrical** sparks crackling around his fingers, comes a **horrific creature** of immense strength and cunning. Created by the obsessive, brilliant medical student Victor Frankenstein, the nameless **monster** is a horrific **mishmash** of reanimated **body parts.**

TIP: Use flames!

The monster hates fire. When locals saw the **creature**, they drove him out with flaming torches, blaming him for killing the old man. Now, the **monster** roams the world in a never-ending search for his creator.

Spare parts

An arm here, a foot there ... Frankenstein stitched his monster together from body parts, stolen from **corpses** in the mortuary or dug out of the ground by **graverobbers.**

It's alive!

Dr Frankenstein used the electricity from a **bolt of lightning** to bring the monster to life, transforming it from a patchwork **cadaver** to a living, thinking being. Horrified by what he had done, the Doctor fled from his own creation.

Friendship is blind

Abandoned in the **wilderness**, the **creature** found protection with an old blind man who could not see its **horrendous** appearance. The monster taught himself to read and think, but when the old man died, the monster grew angry with his creator.

TACTIC: short circuit!

Electrodes on the creature's skull were used to spark its brain into life. Short-circuit them and you may confuse the poor brute long enough to escape without having to fight it.

BEAST RATING

- Enemies: Humanity
- Threat level — 5
- Might in battle — 8
- Difficulty of slaying — 8
- Total — 21

CHAPTER 3

Dragons

With a **thunderous** beating of wings and blasts of **searing flame**, the dragons announce their arrival! Magnificent, **cunning** and vicious, dragons are the mightiest and most dangerous of all **fantastical** beasts, combining an awesome physical threat with magical powers. Some are hungry for **treasure**, but others are just... **hungry!**

6.0

5.0

4.0

3.0

2.0

1.0

LJUBLJANA DRAGON

- Breathing fire within city limits

- Theft of shiny things

- Being overly defensive

CHINESE DRAGON

- Unleashing thunder and lightning for fun

- Flying without wings or a licence

- Becoming invisible at will

Misdemeanours

Dragons

LAMBTON WORM

- Being revoltingly wormlike and evil
- Scoffing sheep
- Fighting knights

JERSEY DEVIL

- Scaring travellers to death
- Vandalising public transport
- Wasting police time by flying away

WYVERN

- Breathing utterly stinky gas
- Spewing foul flames in public
- Posing as a gargoyle

LJUBLJANA DRAGON

Pawing at the ground with **vicious** claws, a ferocious dragon stands watch over the Slovenian city of Ljubljana (say *lyoo-blee-yana*). **Huge wings** beat the air and **smoke** puffs from his nostrils as he looks out for any distant threats to the city built on his **ancient** homeland.

Swamp monster

Folk tales tell how the Greek hero Jason stopped off in Slovenia with his ship, the *Argo*, on the way back from stealing the famous Golden Fleece. He fought and killed a terrible marsh **dragon** living in a lake on the site of the present-day city.

TIP: Don't take treasure

The Ljubljana monster is a typical European dragon - **gigantic**, fire-breathing, four-legged with a scaly hide and **vicious teeth**. Like all of his kind, he has a lust for **gold**, jewels and anything shiny - so best to leave your small change at home!

A powerful friend

Today, the people of Ljubljana see its descendant as their protector - **statues** of him guard the bridge over the Ljubljanica River, and he appears above the **castle** on the city's coat of arms. Don't mess with this city - it's got a **fire-breather** on its side!

Evil twins

Local legends tell of two different types of dragon in this part of Europe – the *zmaj* is **wise** and intelligent, and not always hostile, while the *azdaja* is a **monster** of pure evil. Perhaps the modern dragon is a *zmaj* while Jason fought an *azdaja*?

Dragon Battle

The air is torn by reptilian roars and buildings tumble as the Ljubljana Dragon does mid-air battle with a Chinese Dragon. People flee in panic, for the destruction can be terrible when mighty dragons clash . . . .

LAMBTON WORM

Slithering from the **depths** of the earth comes this huge and **revolting** limbless dragon, known for **terrifying** the villagers of Fatfield in the north of England. **Crushing curls**, a vicious bite, the ability to heal itself instantly ... would you be **brave enough** to take it on?

Hill chill

After ten years, the now **enormous** Worm emerged from the well to **devour** sheep and villagers. It **killed** anyone who attacked it; if they managed to chop bits off, the **monster** just reattached them and healed instantly. It liked to **coil** itself around a local hill; you can still see the marks it left.

Hooked!

According to legend, a young man called John Lambton skipped church one Sunday to go fishing in the River Wear. He **snagged** a **slimy**, worm-like creature that **wriggled** and snapped at his hands ... so he **threw** it down a well.

Well, well ...

When John grew up he went off to seek his fortune as a soldier. Meanwhile, in the well, the Worm grew ... and Grew ... AND GREW.

TACTIC: Be sharp!

John Lambton, now a famous knight, returned to defeat the Worm. On advice of a local witch, he dressed in **spiked** and bladed armour.

BEAST RATING

- Enemies: Knights in armour
- Threat level   8
- Might in battle   7
- Difficulty of slaying   9
- Total   24

Washed away

He lured the Worm back to the river, where it wrapped itself around him - and cut itself to pieces. As lumps of its flesh fell off, they were swept away before the beast could reattach them and heal itself. Finally, the last bloody chunks of the Worm fell from John's armour - the reign of the Worm was over.

WYVERN

Wyverns are one of the smaller types of **dragon**, but what they lack in size they make up for in **nastiness**. These two-legged terrors combine an **evil** temper with sharp **slashing** claws, a poisonous bite and **fiery** breath. They're also fast and agile flyers, so keep an eye on the skies and be ready to **run** for cover!

WEAPON: Flying blowtorch

Specially adapted innards give the Wyvern a **belch** to be reckoned with. They can blow out invisible (but stinky!) poisonous gas, or strike a **spark** on their flinty teeth to ignite their breath in a jet of deadly flames.

Armoured hide

A Wyvern's body is covered in **scales** that protect it from most threats – arrows, spears and even **swords** will just bounce off, unless you can find one of the few **soft** parts in its skin ...

Ancient heritage?

Some people think that Wyverns could be descendants of pterodactyls - flying reptiles that ruled the skies millions of years ago, during the age of the dinosaurs.

Noble symbol

Wyverns are found mostly in western Europe, and particularly in mountainous areas. Back in the olden days, knights in armour would paint a Wyvern on their shield to show they weren't to be messed with.

TIP: Watch the gargoyles!

These dragons are ambush hunters - and they like nothing better than perching on castle battlements (or the top of any old building) pretending to be a stone gargoyle. By the time you realize that the gargoyle is actually moving, it's usually too late!

BEAST RATING

- Enemies: Knights and soldiers
- Threat level   7
- Might in battle   8
- Difficulty of slaying   6
- Total   21

CHAPTER 4

Shapeshifters

With the power to shift from one **deadly** form to another, shapeshifters are the most **dangerously** deceptive **beasts** of all. Combining human intelligence and **cunning** with animal instinct and **strength,** they range from kidnappers and **tricksters** to brutal **predators.** If you hunt one down, be careful - you can never be **quite** sure what you're going to get!

WEREWOLF

Fur shimmering in the **moonlight**, the werewolf emerges from the woods, **blood** and drool dripping from its **slavering** mouth. Lycanthropes have been feared for centuries; when the Full Moon is high in the sky they go on the **prowl**, and don't care whether it's **human** or animal **flesh** on the menu...

TACTIC: Look for bristles

There are various ways to spot a potential Werewolf in between transformations. Eyebrows that meet in the middle and curly fingernails are signs - but plenty of normal people have both of those features, so check for bristles on the suspect's tongue to be sure.

Full Moon

Werewolves are only active for a few nights each month - around the Full Moon. Some say they must actually sleep in the moonlight to be transformed. A person may not realize they are a werewolf until they wake up with raw meat between their teeth ...

TIP: Silver weapons

If you're looking to take down a Werewolf, silver weapons are a must, be they bullets or an axe. But Werewolves have far more strength than any human or wolf, so be very careful when you take your shot, and always have an escape route!

How-to guide

Some strange people deliberately transform themselves into Werewolves. The right potion or ointment can summon this dark magic; sleeping in the Full Moon wearing a belt of wolfskin can also bring about the change.

BEAST RATING

- Enemies: Other Shapeshifters, Vampires
- Threat level   7
- Might in battle   7
- Difficulty of slaying 8
- Total   22

Dangerous bite

Whatever you do, don't let the Werewolf sink his teeth into you – even if you manage to escape alive, it may pass the curse of lycanthropy on to you!

63

KITSUNE

Silent and swift, elegant and cunning, the Kitsune flit in the blink of an eye between the shape of a beautiful woman and their natural, foxy form. Some of these Japanese fox spirits are wise and kindly, many more revel in mischief-making, and some are just plain wicked. So be careful if you cross a Kitsune's path, and watch out for the telltale tail!

WEAPONS: Lightning and lights

Kitsune can spit fire from their mouths or lightning from their tails, usually to defend themselves. But these natural tricksters also use their talents to create eerie lights called "kitsunebe" to lure unwary travellers off their paths.

Foxy faces

Kitsune can take a variety of human forms but most prefer the shape of young women. They often give themselves away through foxlike features, which Japanese people consider to be very beautiful. Alternatively, some Kitsune can actually take possession of people to work their mischief in the human world.

Barking dog

Kitsune hate dogs, and dogs, as a rule, hate Kitsune just as much. They also see straight through their disguises, so if your dog starts barking and snarling, don't be surprised to see that beautiful lady turn back into a fox and run for the hills!

Tell-tails

Shapeshifted Kitsune find it hard to keep their human form, and can give themselves away in several ways. Sometimes they cast a fox's shadow or reflection, and they have trouble hiding their tails, which can pop out at unexpected moments!

Nine-tailed wonders

Kitsune are very long-lived, and as they grow older and wiser, they gain more tails - first one, then five, then seven. The wisest and most **powerful** Kitsune of all have **nine tails**, and are said to be able to see or hear **everything** in the world.

BEAST RATING

- Enemies: None
- Threat level   3
- Might in battle   3
- Difficulty of slaying   2
- Total   8

SKINWALKER

Driving through the Utah desert late at night, something **big** shambles across the road. Is it a bear? A big dog? It stops, stands straight up, and stares right at you ... then is gone, leaving you **frozen** in **terror**. You've just met a **Skinwalker** - a cursed magician that Native Americans have learned to be **very scared** of ...

American outcasts

Many tribes tell tales of the Skinwalkers. The Navajo's stories explain that skinwalkers started out as **shamans** (magicians) who broke the rules of **magic** in their thirst for power. Cast out from society, they now hide in the day and only emerge to **hunt** at night.

Skin-wearers

Skinwalkers have the **power** to transform into many different animals - wolves, foxes, bears and even owls and crows. They **shift** their shape by wrapping themselves in the animal's pelt, and using **forbidden** magical songs. **Transformations** can alter the whole body, or just certain parts.

Deadly stare

Wise Navajo agree that for all his strength, a Skinwalker's **eyes** are his most **dangerous** weapon. Some say that if you make eye contact they can **paralyse** you and drain your life force. Others warn it's even worse - the Skinwalker can take over your **body** and turn you into his puppet!

BEAST RATING

- **Enemies:** All who threaten its people. Werewolves
- **Threat level**   5
- **Might in battle**   8
- **Difficulty of slaying**   9
- **Total**   22

A Skinwalker takes on the abilities of the animal he has changed into – so he may be as fleet-footed as an antelope, as quiet as a fox, or as strong as a bear. Watch out when you're on the track of one, because you never know what form he may take!

TIP:
White ash and name

The only way to kill a Skinwalker face-to-face is to use bullets dipped in white ash from a fire. The Navajo say that if you can find out a Skinwalker's true name, you can use it in a special spell that will rob them of their powers.

FOREST FIGHT

Deep in a wild North American forest, a pack of **Werewolves** – called into their wild and ravenous state by the **eerie** lunar light – attack a bear-spirit **Skinwalker**, but this monstrously powerful 'shifter swings a tree trunk and smashes the **slavering** beasts away as if they were skittles ...

BANSHEE

In the black of the **night**, an unearthly screech sends shivers down your spine. An owl? Maybe a fox? You'd better hope it wasn't the wail of the **Banshee**, whose screams foretell **violent death!** Driven half-mad by their visions of the **bloody** future, they won't be reasoned with or silenced. Best stick in your earplugs – and hide!

Ancient walls

Some haunt **castles** or stately homes, where their screams are said to foretell a **death** in the family. The Banshee sometimes appears wandering along battlements, **tearing** at her clothes in grief.

TIP: Cover your ears!

The Banshee's **cry** varies. In the west of Ireland it's said to be a low and **melodic** song, but in the east, it's a **piercing screech** loud enough to shatter glass. So if in doubt, cover your ears!

Animal forms

Like all **fairies**, Banshees can shapeshift to take the form of animals – usually stoats, weasels or hares. Their favourite form, however, is the **hooded crow**, which haunts wild woods and high mountains, and flocks to **battlefields** to feast on the flesh of the dead.

HABITAT: Ancient haunts

The word "ban-shee" means "woman of the burial mounds" and Banshees are often found around ancient **grave mounds** in Britain and especially Ireland. Sometimes, you may stumble across them washing bloody clothes and **armour** in nearby rivers ...

Banshees are the wildest of the fairy folk
- although they can shapeshift to appear
as beautiful girls with butterfly wings.
When they let the illusion slip they
reveal their true form - tattered and
ragged wings, worn and haggard
features, and staring, hypnotic eyes.

BEAST RATING

- **Enemies: None**
- **Threat level**   4
- **Might in battle**   1
- **Difficulty of slaying**   9
- **Total**   14

CHAPTER 5

Trolls, Giants AND Demons

Barren mountaintops and ancient woods are haunted by **creatures** far older than humanity – **elemental** beings from the **First Age of the Earth.** Some like nothing more than to meddle in the affairs of man, while others prefer to keep their distance in the remote wilderness. But all can be **deadly** when angered, and you cross them at your **peril!**

3.0

2.5

2.0

1.5

1.0

0.5

0.0

DRAUG

- Slaughtering mortals and stealing cattle
- Throwing curses
- Entering dreams without permission

BLACK SHUCK

- Making graveyards no-go areas
- Damaging church property
- Howling after 11pm

JOTUN FROST GIANT

- Bringing winter five months early
- Freezing mortals to death
- Associating with renegade Norse gods

Crimes and Misdemeanours

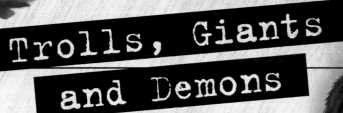

Trolls, Giants and Demons

KRAMPUS

- Kidnapping kids at Christmas
- Swapping presents for coal
- Terrifying children for fun

ELF

- Slaughtering Trolls (even useful ones)
- Being madly mischievous
- Battling and brawling

TROLL

- Stealing and eating goats
- Fighting Elves
- Being grumpy in charge of a bridge

DRAUG

Draugs are Viking **warriors** risen from the **dead**, anchored to the Earth by the fortune they pillaged in life. They cheated death to guard their riches, thus becoming stinking, demon **zombies**. They hate mortals and will kill any they see on their nightly roamings. Your only hope: track and **kill them first!**

Stinky strength

The Draug may be little more than **rotting flesh** and bone, but he has the strength of ten fighting men. He can morph into a foul smoke, rising at will from his grave.

WEAPON: Magic axe

The Draug's weapon, a special "skeggox", or bearded axe, will cleave a mortal in two. Charms, written in **runic** script, bestow **magical** properties in combat, the axe seeking and targeting an opponent's weakest point.

TIP: Scissors and spells

Iron scissors left open on the corpse's chest will cut the soul and stop them becoming a Draug; and to stop a Draug haunting your nightmares, carve a spell on a stone and hurl it on the grave.

Tie the big toes together to stop him walking.

Rode rage

There is no sight more terrifying than a Draug on the rampage. They steal bulls for the thrill of it, riding the snorting creatures into **demented** frenzy. Some say it is the Draug's smell that torments them; others the pain of the rattling **bones** on their back. The bulls are **dead** by dawn.

TRACKING: Follow the stench!

The demon Draug leaves no tracks where he passes. But you can **smell** him a mile distant. When the air is thick with an **evil stench,** you know a Draug is close. Follow his foul scent to **hunt** him down.

Dried twigs hidden in the clothes may suck up evil desires.

TO VANQUISH:
Attack and behead it

Leap at it with a longsword and **sever its head.** Bury it at a crossroads and burn the **body** on a pyre. Only then is the Draug truly **dead.**

BEAST RATING

- Enemies: Mortals
- Threat level — 8
- Might in battle — 8
- Difficulty of slaying — 7
- Total — 23

BLACK SHUCK

What's that in the **darkness?** A whisper-quiet padding of **huge paws**, an unearthly howl, the glow of **flaming** eyes - and the **demon-dog Black Shuck** is on you in an instant!. Whether it's a warner of **imminent death**, or just a watcher over **souls** in graveyards, this dog's bite is worse than its **bark!**

WEAPON: Burning claws

The Shuck's claws are **vicious.** Some believe they can be **scorchingly hot!**

HABITAT: Graves and lanes

Black Shucks have terrified village dwellers in Northern Europe for centuries. They **prowl** around dark lanes and **graveyards,** lurking amongst the shadows and **misty hollows ...**

WARNING: Storm signs

Their appearance is often foreshadowed by sudden **storms** - with **lightning** strikes. (The Shuck can cause as much destruction as lightning itself. In 1577, one **destroyed** a church steeple.)

A Shuck's hideous howl will make your blood run cold. If you hear one, you'd best shut your eyes; seeing a Shuck may mean you will meet a hideous fate!

The burnt slashes on this church door (in a village called Bungay) were made by a Black Shuck's hot claws; locals call the burns "the Devil's scorch marks".

BEAST RATING

- Enemies: Mortals
- Threat level   6
- Might in battle   8
- Difficulty of slaying   9
- Total   23

JOTUN FROST GIANT

There's a sudden **chill**. You can see your breath turn to ice in the **eerie** mist. Then **lumbering** from the fog comes an enormous figure - a Jotun Frost Giant. These **fearsome warriors** are used to taking on gods, so your only hope is to run - and don't "**freeze**"!

HABITAT:
Icy heights

The Jotun homeland of Jotünheim is **hidden** among high mountains. To reach it you'll have to fight your way through dense, **scratching** forests.

Jack frost

As their clothing suggests, the Frost Giants are **freezing** to the touch - when they descend from their mountain home each winter, they bring their **icy cold** into the world of men.

Frost Giant central

The Giants are mostly **loners**, but on rare occasions, they gather for **feasts** in the great hall of their king Thrymr - be careful, though, or you might end up on the menu!

WEAPON:
Mighty club

Frost Giants use huge clubs to fight Norse gods such as Thor - or to flatten **puny** mortals!

Figure in the fog

They are often glimpsed as vast, **sinister shapes** in distant mountain mists and **impenetrable fog.**

Viking soothsayers tell that one day the Jotun will descend from their mountain lairs, spreading icy winter across the world. The great ash tree Yggdrasil, which supports the world, will shake, heralding Ragnarok, the devastating final battle between the Jotun and the Norse gods.

BEAST RATING

- Enemies: Norse gods, mortals
- Threat level — 8
- Might in battle — 9
- Difficulty of slaying — 9
- Total — 26

KRAMPUS

Ho ho... **NO!** The Krampus is on his way, wishing you a not-so-happy holiday! This demon from the highest Alpine mountains is Santa's evil twin. It punishes **naughty** children and terrifies good ones! If you hear his chains on **Christmas Eve**, bury your head in the pillow – and don't peek out!

Naughty or nice?

The Krampus turns up at the same time as Santa – but while good kids get presents from Santa's bag of goodies, bad children get stuffed into the Krampus's sack and carried away to **his lair**.

WARNING: Rattling racket

While Santa's arrival is announced by gentle sleigh bells, the Krampus wraps himself in **chains** and rusty cowbells to scare children. Cover your ears to **protect yourself!**

WEAPON: Whip or twigs

The Krampus carries a bundle of birch twigs which he uses to beat **naughty** children. Sometimes he even leaves the bundle behind, pinned to a wall as a reminder to be good next year!

TRACKING:
Cloven prints

The Krampus's hairy legs and cloven hooves show his beastly nature – you may be able to track him from his goatlike footprints in the snow, but make sure he doesn't spot you as he'll easily run you down.

Black Christmas

Children who aren't bad enough to be beaten or dragged off in the Krampus's sack, but aren't good enough to get presents, wake up to find their Christmas stockings have been stuffed – with coal!

BEAST RATING

- Enemies: Naughty children
- Threat level   5
- Might in battle   4
- Difficulty of slaying 6
- Total   15

ELF

Most Elves are mean-spirited, mischievous and downright dangerous. Armed to the teeth, athletic and fast-moving, they have keen eyesight and hearing and will spot you long before you see them. Our advice? Be polite, watch out for tricks, and if all else fails, carry something shiny and expensive - Elves love treasure!

TRACKING: Fairy rings

Elves love a raucous party, chasing each other in circles at dawn and dusk, and leaving these distinctive rings of mushrooms to mark the trails of their dancing. Don't be mislead by the name "fairy ring" - there's nothing fairy-like about them!

Shapeshifters

There are many different types of Elf and related creatures - some looking beautiful and some demonic. But whatever their appearance, all Elves are troublesome, unpredictable and violent creatures underneath.

TACTIC: Make your mark

When they're not fighting, Elves love to play tricks - but they can only enter your house if they're invited. Drawing this Elf cross on your front door warns them that they're not welcome and protects you from their mischief.

BEAST RATING

- Enemies: Mortals, Trolls
- Threat level   7
- Might in battle   6
- Difficulty of slaying   7
- Total   20

One favourite trick of the Elves is to kidnap human babies from their cradles, switching them for their own elvish young.

WEAPON: Knives

Elves are ferocious fighters, always spoiling for a battle and armed to the hilt. Kitted out with the vicious blades, they'll slice and dice anyone they don't like the look of – whether that's a human, a Troll or another Elf.

War of the Elves

As the Elf clans swarm onto the plain, the battle reaches fever pitch, corpses mingling with the churned mud below. As sabres clash, a filthy Troll rises up from his underground lair, spitting Elf blood and guts...

TROLL

Nasty, brutish, tall and ugly, Trolls are **enormous**, **ferocious** and always hungry! If you're venturing into troll territory you'd better take a goat in case one catches your scent. The best time to go Troll hunting is just before dawn - they're **creatures** of the night, and tend to "go to pieces" in **daylight!**

Favourite snack

Trolls are famously **greedy** - they'll eat anything, but **goat meat** is their favourite food of all. Leave an unguarded goat tethered in Troll territory, and there won't be much left the following day!

Deadly sniffers

These beefy giants may be famously slow-witted, but they have an incredible **sense of smell,** and can sniff out humans over several miles. The smell of Christians, who drove them away from their traditional lands, makes them particularly **mad.**

Deadly sunrise

Most Trolls are **night hunters**, retreating to caves or under their bridges during the day. For some species, this is just because they prefer the night, but if certain types of troll are caught in **direct sunlight**, a chemical reaction **can turn them to stone.**

TACTIC: **Ring out!**

Trolls don't like **loud noises**, and in particular they hate the sound of church bells. Take a small one with you for protection on any **Troll-hunting** expeditions.

HABITAT: **Bridges and hollows**

Trolls like to make their homes **under bridges**, which provide shade in the daytime, a ready supply of water, and a good place to lie in wait for **unwary travellers.**

BEAST RATING

- Enemies: Mortals, Elves
- Threat level   8
- Might in battle   9
- Difficulty of slaying   7
- Total   24

GLOSSARY

ATHENIANS - people of Athens, Greece.

AZDAJA - a vile, cruel East European dragon of pure evil.

AZTECS - the people of old central Mexico, from between the 14th and 17th centuries. They created a powerful, colourful civilization, and built great cities with astonishing temples and pyramids.

BANSHEE - a type of terrifying female spirit from Ireland, famed for its blood-chilling wail.

BLACK SHUCK - an English demon-dog.

BOKOR - a Voodoo priest.

CADAVER - a dead body.

CENTAURS - half-human, half-horse warriors from Ancient Greek myth.

CHIMU, OR CHIN-MU - the magical bumps on a Chinese Dragon's head which give these wingless wonders the power of flight.

CLOVEN HOOF - a hoof divided down the middle into two parts, such as that of a goat ... or a devil.

CRETE - a Greek island in the eastern Mediterranean Sea, site of the Minoan civilization.

CYCLOPS - a massive one-eyed giant from ancient Greek myths.

DEVIL - a beast of pure evil, usually with horns, a tail and cloven hooves.

DEITY - a god.

DRAGON - a monstrous reptile, usually capable of flying and breathing fire, sometimes with four legs, sometimes with none, but always fierce.

DRAUG - an undead Viking warrior.

ELF - a small, skilled and vicious race of supernatural beast, often mistakenly thought to be nice.

GARGOYLE - a hideous and fantastic dragon-like monster, shown in stone on many old churches and other buildings.

GORGON - one of three sisters - Stheno, Euryale, and Medusa - from ancient Greek myth, with snakes for hair and the power to turn men to stone with a glance.

GREEK HEROES - the strong, brave and clever warriors of ancient Greek myths, who managed to defeat many a monster, using cunning and help from their gods.

HABITAT - the place a beast likes to dwell.

HINDU - belonging to Hinduism, a religion from India, full of extraodinary stories and deities.

IMPALE - to stick a stake or other large sharp object through something - or some beast.

JIANG SHI - a Chinese hopping zombie.

JOTUN FROST GIANT - gigantic icy mega-monsters of Norse myth.

KITSUNE - magical Japanese foxes capable of taking human form.

KRAMPUS - a devilish beast that appears in countries around the Alps, infamous for punishing and scaring children in the festive season.

LABYRINTH - the complicated maze built for King Minos as a place to keep the Minotaur.

LYCANTHROPE - the scientific name for a Werewolf; lycanthropy is the power to turn into a wolf.

MINOAN - belonging to this ancient civilization from Crete, ruled by King Minos.

MINOTAUR - the part-bull, part-man beast that dwelled in the labyrinth.

MISDEMEANOURS - acts of appalling behaviour or mischief.

MORTALS - normal human beings - such as you ... ?

MYTH - an ancient story so old and mysterious that no one knows what part of it is made up and what is true.

NAGA - a spirit or beast from Hindu and Buddhist myth, often female, that combines human features with those of a serpent.

NAVAJO - a Native American Indian people, from the lands we now call New Mexico and Arizona.

NORSE - of ancient Scandinavia, especially the Vikings. Norse myths are full of huge strong heroes, enormous ultra-powerful beasts and mighty deities.

PETRIFYING - usually used to just mean very frightening, this word actually means something that is turning - or can turn you - into stone.

PHYSICIAN - a doctor.

REPELLENTS - substances that drive a being away, such as garlic to a vampire.

SELKIE - sea beast from waters of the coastal islands around Scotland. Selkies live as seals in the sea but transform into women when on land.

SERPENT - a snake or similar reptile, usually evil.

SHAPESHIFTER - a human with the ability to become an animal.

SKINWALKER - in Native American Indian myth, a person with the power to transform into any animal he or she desires.

SLOVENIA - a Central European state. Its capital city is Ljubljana.

SUPERNATURAL - something that is "above nature" and beyond normal explanation, such as a magical power or being.

TACTIC - a way to approach a problem or difficult task ... such as defeating a beast.

TROLL - a large, grumpy, lumpy, ugly beast, usually dwelling in a cave or under a bridge.

UNDEAD - a being that once died but now lives again in a horrid, deathlike state.

VAMPIRE - a being that feeds on living creatures, usually by drinking their blood.

VENOM - a naturally made poison, usually squirted at or injected into its victims.

VIKINGS - the fierce pirate traders and raiders from Scandinavia who caused havoc on the coasts of Northern Europe between the 8th and 11th centuries.

WEREWOLF - a human partly or totally transformed into a wolf.

WYVERN - a smaller species of dragon, possibly venomous, sometimes fire-breathing, often shown on shields.

XOLOTL - the dog-headed Aztec god of lightning and death who protects the Sun.

YGGDRASIL - in Norse myth, the great tree of life that supports this and all worlds.

ZMAJ - a wise Eastern European dragon, fierce but fair.

INDEX

A
Achilles 22
Anubis 38, 93
archery 13, 22
arrows 13, 22
Asia 7, 20, 23
Athena 12
Athenians 10, 92
axes 10-11, 62, 78
azdaja 47, 92
Aztecs 8, 14, 92, 93

B
Banshees 61, 72-73, 92
birch twigs 84
Black Shuck 76, 80-81, 92
blades 21
blood 26, 28
bokors 36, 37, 92
brains 37
bulls 10, 11, 79

C
canopic jars 39
Caribbean 36
cats 32
caves 16, 33, 91, 94
Centaurs 9, 18-19, 22-23, 92
Central America 14
children 8, 55, 77, 84, 85
China 32, 48-49
Chinese dragons 44, 48-49, 50-51, 92
Chiron 22
Christmas 77, 84, 85, 93
claws 46, 49, 56, 80, 81
clubs 17, 83
cobras, king 20
coffins 29, 32, 38
Crete 10, 11, 92
crimes and misdemeanours 8-9,
    26-27, 44-45, 60-61, 76-77, 92
Cyclops 9, 16-19, 92

D
demons 14, 15, 75, 78-79, 80-81,
    84-85, 86, 92
dinosaurs 57
dogs 38, 66, 80-81, 92
Dracula 26, 28-31
dragons 42-57, 92, 93
Draug 76, 78-79, 93
drugs 37

E
Egypt 30, 38
electricity 40, 41
elves 77, 86-89, 91, 93
England 52
Euryale 12, 93
eyes 12, 16, 68, 73, 80, 92

F
fairies 72, 73, 86
finfolk 64, 65
fire 40, 44, 46, 66, 93
fog 82, 83
foxes 66, 93
Frankenstein's Monster 27, 40-41
frost 82

G
gargoyles 45, 57, 93
giants 16-19, 34-35, 74-75, 90-91, 92
    Jotun Frost Giant 76, 82-83, 92
gods
    Monsters of the Gods 6-23
    Norse gods 76, 83
Golems 26, 34-35
Gorgons 8, 12-13, 93
graves and graveyards 24, 37, 72,
    76, 78, 80
graverobbers 40
    see also tombs
Greece 7, 10, 12, 13, 16, 22, 23, 92
    Greek myths 16, 17, 22, 46, 93

H
hairstyles 8, 12
Haiti 36
Hindu myths 21, 93, 94
hooves, cloven 55, 85, 93
horses 22-23
Hungary 28

I
ice 82
India 20, 21, 93
Ireland 72, 92
islands 16, 36, 64, 65

J
Japan 66, 93
Jason 46, 47
Jersey Devil 45, 54-55
Jews 34, 35
Jiang Shi 26, 32-33, 93
Jotun Frost Giant 76, 82-83, 93

K
Kitsune 61, 66-67, 93
knives 87
Knossos 10
Krampus 77, 84-85, 93

L
labyrinths 10, 93
Lambton, John 52, 53
Lambton Worm 45, 52-53
lightning 8, 14, 32, 40, 44, 66,
    80, 95
Ljubljana dragon 44, 46-47, 50-51
Loew, Rabbi 34, 35

M
mazes 10, 11
Mediterranean Sea 16, 92
Medusa 12, 13, 93
Mekong River 20
Mictlan 14
Minoans 11, 92, 93
Minos, King 10, 93
Minotaur 8, 10-11, 93
mirrors 13, 28
misdemeanours 94
    see also crimes and misdemeanours
Monsters of the Gods 6-23
moonlight 62
mountains 82, 84, 93
Mummies 27, 30-31, 38-39
myths 16, 21, 22, 46, 92, 93, 94, 95

N
Naga 9, 20-21, 94
Native Americans 54, 68, 94
naughty children 84, 85
Navajo 68, 94
New Jersey 54
Norse gods 76, 83, 93, 94, 95
North America 54, 70

O
Odysseus 17
Orkney Islands 64, 65

P
Perseus 13, 22
pharaohs 38
Polyphemus 17
potions 36
Prague 34, 35
pterodactyls 57
pyramids 38, 92

Q
Qing Dynasty 32

R
reflections 13, 28, 32
resurrection 39
rivers 20, 21, 46, 52, 53
Romania 28

S
sacrifice 10
Sagittarius 22
salt 37
Santa 84
sarcophagi 38, 39
Scotland 64, 94
sealskins 64, 65
Selkies 60, 64-65, 94
Shapeshifters 58-73, 86, 94
Shuck, Black 76, 80-81, 92

skinwalkers 61, 68-71, 94
Slovenia 46, 94
smell 8, 16, 78, 79, 90
snakes 12, 20
South America 7
Stheno 12, 93
storms 48
    see also lightning; thunder
synagogues 34

T
teeth 46, 56, 62, 63
Tepes, Vlad 28
Thailand 20
Theseus 10
thunder 14, 44
tombs 27, 30, 38, 39
    see also graves and graveyards
trances 37
Transylvania 28
treasure 42, 46
trolls 74-75, 77, 87, 88-89,
    90-91, 94

U
Undead, the 24-41, 94
underworld 14
Utah 68

V
vampires 28, 29, 94
Vikings 78, 93, 94, 95
Vlad Dracula see Dracula
voodoo 36, 92

W
weapons 10-11, 13, 14, 17, 21, 22, 56,
    62, 66, 78, 80, 83, 84, 87, 88-89
werewolves 60, 62-63, 70-71, 95
wine 22
Wyverns 45, 56-57, 95

X
Xolotl 8, 14-15, 95

Z
zmaj 47, 95
Zombies 27, 32, 36-37, 78, 93